The King's Wish

AND OTHER STORIES

by BENJAMIN ELKIN

Illustrated by LEONARD SHORTALL

Beginner Books

THE KING'S WISH

The King of Tam was a very good King. All day and every day he rode around Tam. He had to see that all were well and happy.

One day the King saw a
man with some fish. The King
said, "Oh, it must be fun to
fish! How I wish I had time
to fish."

The three sons of the King
heard his wish. Son One heard
it. Son Two heard it. And Son
Three heard it too.

That night the three sons
went to see the King.

Son One said, "Father, we
heard your wish. We want you
to have time to fish. Go and
fish! We will do your work."

The King said, "Why, you
are just boys! But maybe you
could do a King's work. Let
us find out. I will give you a
test—a King Test."

"Come with me," said the
King. "I will take you to the
King Test Room."

Now the three sons were in
the King Test Room. They
looked all around. Then the
King called to them. "I have
shut this door. This is the test.
You must not open this door.
But you must get out of the
room. Can you do it?"

Could they do it? They saw there was just one door. The King had said they could not open that door. Then how could they get out? Son One said, "We will have to find some other way."

"Look," said Son One. "Maybe we can get out that way. Let us try."

Son Three got up on top of Son Two. Son One got up on top of Son Three. Now Son One could see out. "We can not get out this way," said Son One. "We are all too big. We will have to find another way."

13

But could they find another
way out? Son Two and Son
Three looked way down low.
All they found was a hole. It
was just a little mouse hole.

Son One said, "Look! I
found something. I found some
red ink. Maybe we can get
out with this."

Son One told the other sons,
"This ink will help us to get
out. We can do the King Test
now! The King's man will look
in here. He will see us."

Soon the King's man did
look in the King Test Room.

"Open that door!" the King's
man called. "Open that door!
The King's sons are in there. I
see that they are sick. Get the
King!"

The men opened the door.
They ran into the King Test
Room. They saw the King's
sons. The sons had red spots
all over them. They looked
very sick.

The men took the sons right
out of the room.

Right out of the door. And then. . .

The King saw that his sons
were out of the room. He saw
that the spots were just red
ink. He said, "You did it!
You got out of the room and
you did not open the door.
My men did!"

Then the King said, "You
are just boys. But you can do
a king's work. I name you all
kings."

Then the King said good-by
to his sons. "Thank you," he
said. "You gave me my wish.
Now I can go away. Now I
can fish."

HOW A SQUIRREL HELPED
THE KING

The King had been away
for a long time. What fun he
had had! It was fun to catch
fish. It was fun to see the birds.

Then one day he saw a
little squirrel.

"Oh, oh," said the King.

"What is this?" The head
of this squirrel is caught in
the tree. He cannot get it out."

Then the King walked up
to the tree.

He let the little squirrel out.

But he did not see two men
in back of him.

The men came up in back
of the King.

They put a big net right
over his head.

"Help!" said the King.
"They want my fish. Let me
out of here!"

The squirrel saw what was going on.

He did not like it.

He thought, "The King helped me. Now I must help him."

The squirrel hit the men.

He hit the men with nuts.

Bump! A big nut hit one man on the head.

Bump! A big nut hit the other man on the head.

"You hit me," said one
man.

"No, you hit me," said the
other.

Then the two men hit one
another.

This was just what the squirrel wanted. He jumped down from the tree.

In no time at all he had a big hole in that net.

In no time at all, the King was out!

The men did not see him.

Now the King wanted to get

the two men.

But how could he do it?

The King came up in back
of the men. Down came the
big net. Down went the men.
But could the King hold
them?

A wagon was coming.

But it was far away.

"Hurry, hurry," the King
called. "I have bad men here!
I can not hold them long."

The men in the wagon
made the horses hurry.
Fast. . . faster.

They got there in time.

They put the bad men in
the wagon. "We will take
them away," the wagon men
said. "We are glad we could
help you, good King."

Then the King said, "Thank
you, little squirrel. That was a
good thing you did for me.
Tomorrow I am going home. I
will take you home to Tam
with me."

THE BIG FIRE

The next day, the King was
up before the sun. He was
happy. He was on his way
home. But all at once, he saw
something far away. It looked
like a fire!

There was a big fire in
Tam. A big house was on fire.

But no one in Tam saw the
fire. "Oh!" said the King.
"They are all fast asleep!"

The King said, "I must do
something fast!" He had three
arrows. He took one of them
out.

"I must hit the town bell
with this arrow," said the
King. "I must wake some one
up! I must wake up my sons!"

The King let the arrow fly.
But the arrow did not hit the
bell. It fell in the lake. Now
one of the King's three arrows
was gone. And now another
big house was on fire!

"I must wake some one! I must wake my sons!" said the King. The King let another arrow fly.

But this arrow fell into the
fire. And now three big houses
were on fire.

Now the King had just one
arrow. His very last arrow! A
very big arrow! The King said,
"I must hit that bell! I must
wake up some one in my
town!" He let the big arrow
fly.

It did hit the bell!

Would the King's sons hear
it?

Would some one in all of
Tam wake up?

55

The King's sons did hear it!
Now, at last, they did wake
up!

The King's sons ran out.

"Get water! Get water!"
they called.

The King's sons told every
one just what to do. It took a
long time. And it took a lot of
water.

But, at last, the big fire of
Tam was out. "We did it!"
said Son Two. "We put out
that fire. We are very good
kings."

But then Son One found the
arrow. He found the big arrow
of the King.

"Look," he said. "It was our father who hit the bell! We were fast asleep. He had to wake us up! I guess we were not very good kings after all!"

Then the sons saw the King coming. "Father," they said. "We were not good kings."

"Yes, you were," said the King. "You are just boys. But you did what you could. From now on you will work with me."

All in the town of Tam
heard this. And all in the
town of Tam were happy.